Patterns

Published by LDA
an imprint of

Editors: Melissa Warner Hale, Susan Fitzgerald

Published by LDA
An imprint of McGraw-Hill Children's Publishing

Send all inquiries to:
McGraw-Hill Children's Publishing
3195 Wilson Drive NW
Grand Rapids, Michigan 49544

Patterns—grades K—4
ISBN: 0-7424-1928-2

1 2 3 4 5 6 7 8 9 MAL 09 08 07 06 05 04

The McGraw-Hill Companies

Table of Contents

Introduction

The activities in this book will help students of any age or ability level become adept at naming, recognizing, and extending patterns. A range of activities will appeal to different learning styles. Visual learners will enjoy the artwork as well as many coloring and drawing opportunities. "Say It" prompts encourage auditory learners to verbalize what they have learned. Kinesthetic learners will benefit from movement exercises, arranging pattern blocks, building models, and cut-and-paste activities.

Multiple representations of patterns will help students identify patterns in the world around them. Repeating patterns are demonstrated using colors, sizes, motions, sounds, and pictures. Stories, pictures, and models illustrate various growing and decreasing patterns. Pattern blocks connect these concepts to geometry.

Extension Activities

- Students can verbalize, act out, and make repeating patterns. Encourage them to say the pattern using characteristics (large, small, large, small) and to name the pattern using letters (ABAB). Discuss how the same pattern can look different if it starts in a different place (ABBABB vs. BABBABB). Have students make the same pattern by drawing, lining up common objects, or performing a sequence of actions (clapping, stomping, jumping, etc.).
- Make connections between pattern-block exercises and geometric concepts. Ask students how different arrangements resemble objects such as fish, butterflies, or rockets. See if students can find repeating patterns used at home and school (wallpaper borders, tile floors, etc.).
- Each growing and decreasing pattern can be modeled by counting forward or backward on a 100 chart. Students can compare 2 different patterns by using different colors on the same chart. Choose a growing or decreasing pattern from one of the activities in this book. Allow each student to choose a starting number. Each student should color the pattern on the chart. Then compare charts. Discuss how the patterns are the same and how they are different. Ask students to create a model or make up a story to match their patterns.

Name ______________________________ Date ______________

AB Patterns

Directions: Color the Hippos. Complete the pattern.
G = Green, Y = Yellow, R = Red, B = Blue

1.

2.

3.

Say It

Say the patterns out loud. How are the patterns the same?
Make your own pattern of the same type.

0-7424-1928-2 *Patterns*

Name ______________________ Date ______________________

AB Patterns

Directions: Cut out the squares at the bottom of the page. Paste them in the empty boxes to complete the patterns.

1.

2.

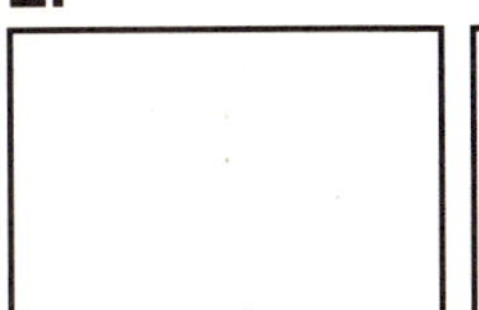     

3.

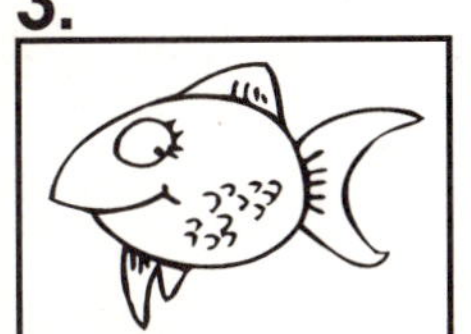     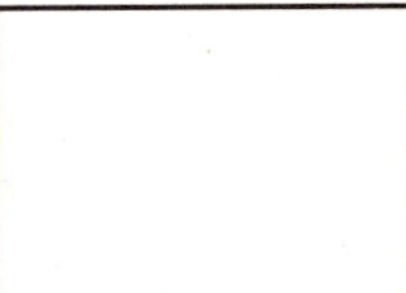

Say It

How are the patterns the same?
Make a pattern like these using claps and stomps.

Name ______________________________ Date ______________

AB Patterns

Directions: Use pattern blocks. Match the shapes. Name the pattern. Color to record.

1\.

2.

3. Make your own pattern. Trace the shapes. Color to record.

 **Say It**

Say the patterns out loud. Use the words **triangle**, **square**, and **diamond**. How are the patterns the same?

Name ______________________ Date ______________________

AB Patterns

Directions: Use pattern blocks. Match the shapes. Name the pattern. Color to record.

1.

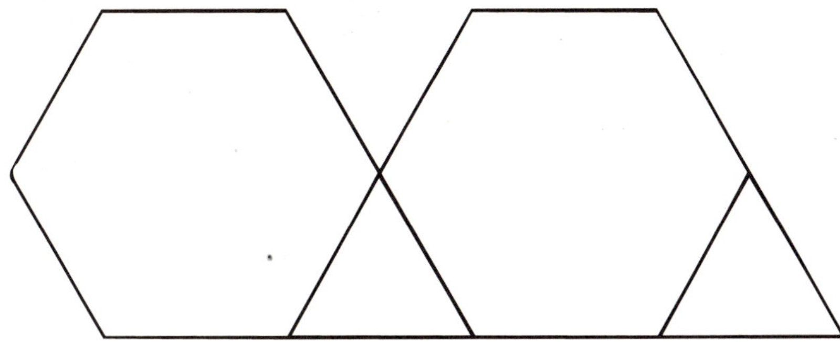

2.

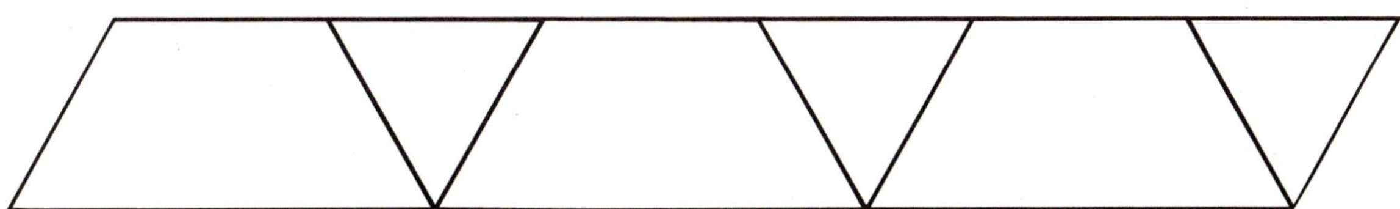

3. Make your own pattern. Trace the shapes. Color to record.

Say It

Say the patterns out loud. Use the words **triangle**, **hexagon**, and **trapezoid**. How are the patterns the same?

0-7424-1928-2 *Patterns*

Name ______________________ Date ______________

AB Patterns

Directions: Use pattern blocks. Match the shapes. Name the pattern. Color to record.

1.

---------------- ----------------

2.

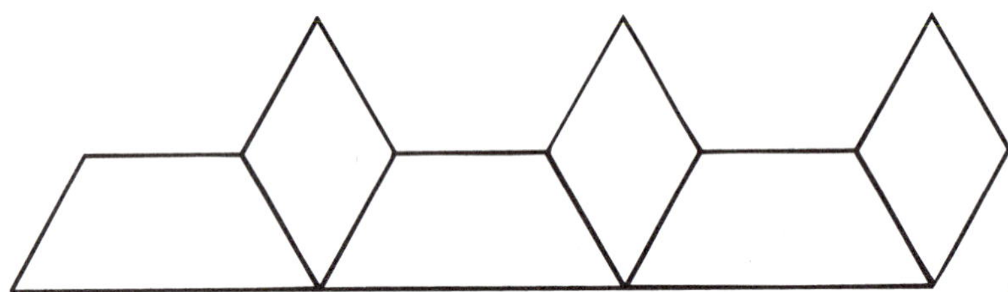

---------------- ----------------

3.

---------------- ----------------

Say It

How many different shapes are used in each pattern? Name the patterns.

Name ______________________________ Date ______________

ABB Patterns

Directions: Act out the patterns. Repeat the patterns.

1\.

stomp	clap	clap	stomp	clap	clap

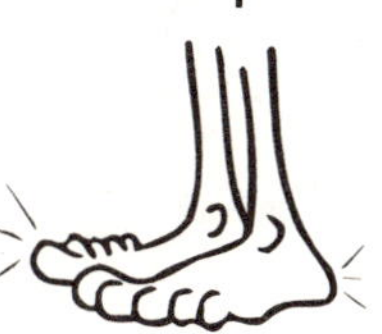

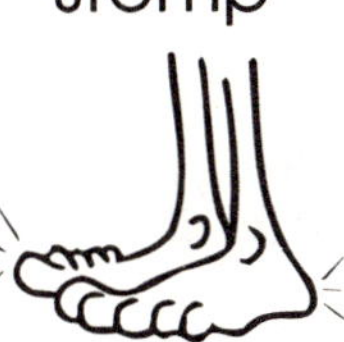

2\.

3\.

kick left	kick right	kick right	kick left	kick right	kick right

Say It

Sing the pattern. How is it the same as the other patterns on this page?

la mi mi la mi mi la mi mi

Name ______________________ Date ______________

ABB Patterns

Directions: Color the horses. Complete the patterns.
R = Red, B = Blue, O = Orange, P = Purple

1.

2.

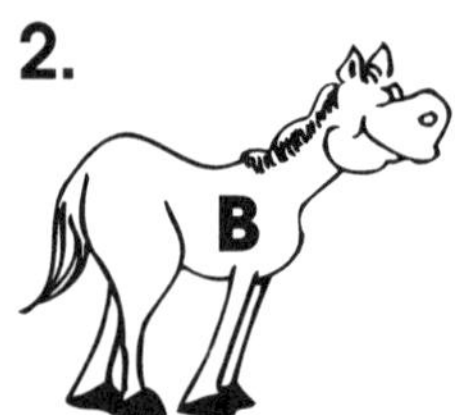

3.

Say It

Say the patterns out loud. How are the patterns the same?
Make your own pattern of the same type.

0-7424-1928-2 *Patterns*

Name ______________________________ Date ____________________

ABB Patterns

Directions: Use pattern blocks. Match the shapes. Complete the pattern. Color to record.

1.

2.

3.

Say It

How many different shapes are used in each pattern?
Were any shapes repeated to make the pattern?
Name the pattern.

Name ______________________ Date ____________

AABB Patterns

Directions: Cut out the squares at the bottom of the page. Paste them in the empty boxes to complete the patterns.

1.

2.

3.

   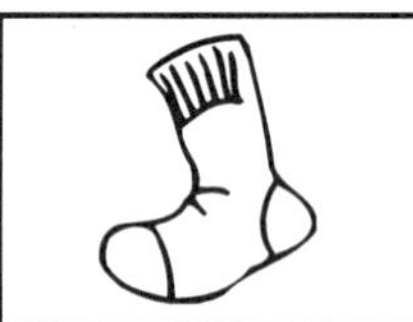  

 **Say It**

How are the patterns the same?
Make a pattern like these using claps and stomps.

   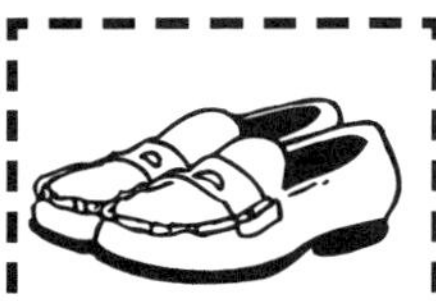

Name ______________________________ Date ______________

AABB Pattern

Directions: Act out the patterns. Repeat the patterns.

1.

stomp stomp clap clap stomp stomp clap clap

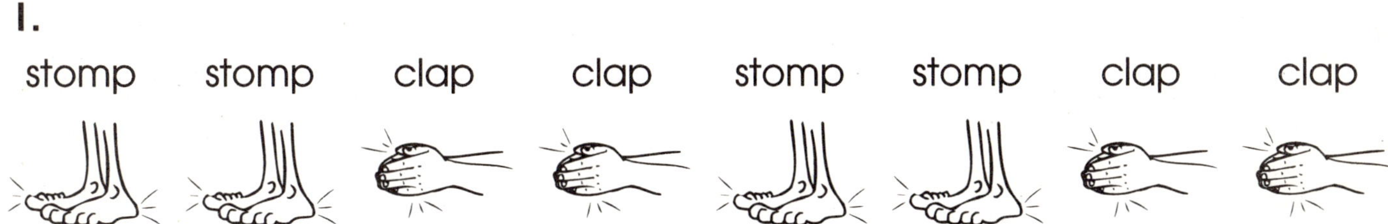

2.

3.

jump jump sit-down sit-down jump jump sit-down sit-down

Say It

Sing the pattern. How is it the same as the other patterns on this page?

la la mi mi la la mi mi la la mi mi

Name ______________________________ Date ____________________

ABC Patterns

Directions: Copy the patterns. Make the motions and say the words. Repeat the patterns.

1.

rock	paper	scissors	rock	paper	scissors

2.

paper	scissors	rock	paper	scissors	rock

3.

paper	rock	scissors	paper	rock	scissors

Say It

How are the patterns alike?
Which patterns have the same order?
Which patterns have a different order?

Name ______________________________ Date ____________________

ABC Patterns

Directions: Cut out the squares at the bottom of the page. Paste them in the empty boxes to complete the patterns.

1.

2.

    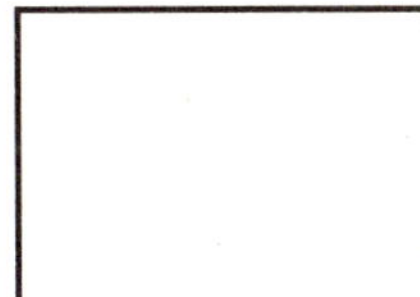 

3.

Say It

Say the patterns out loud. Use the words **small**, **medium**, and **large**. Which patterns have the same order?

Name ______________________________ Date ______________

ABC Patterns

Directions: Use pattern blocks. Match the shapes. Name the pattern. Color to record.

1.

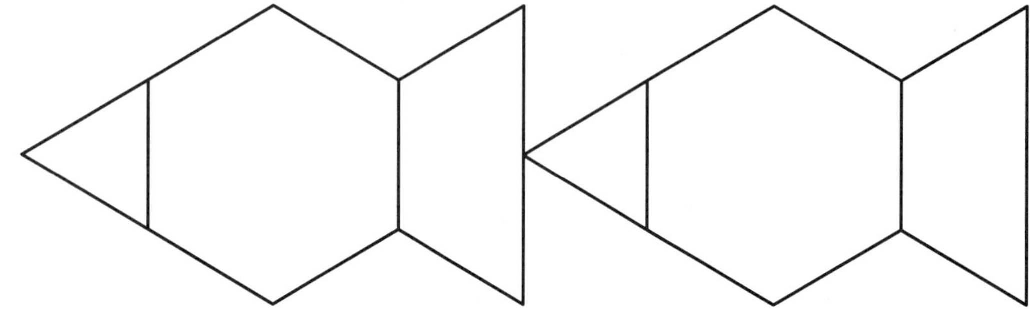

2.

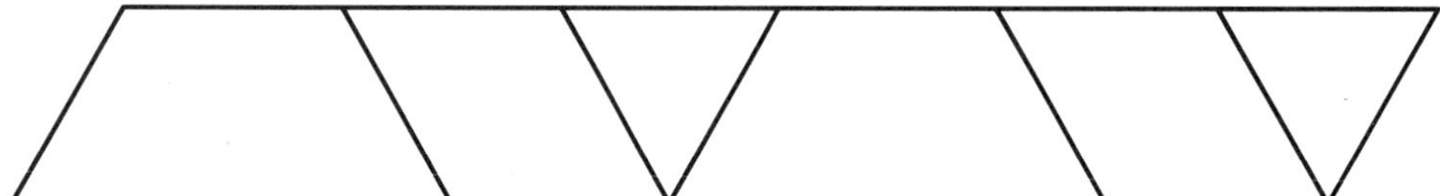

3. Make your own pattern. Trace the shapes. Color to record.

Say It

How are these patterns the same?
How are they different?

Name ______________________ Date ______________

ABC Patterns

Directions: Use pattern blocks. Match the shapes. Complete the pattern. Color to record.

1.

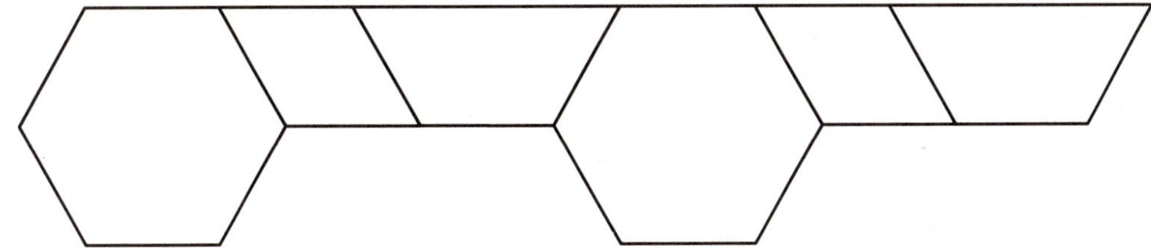

____

2.

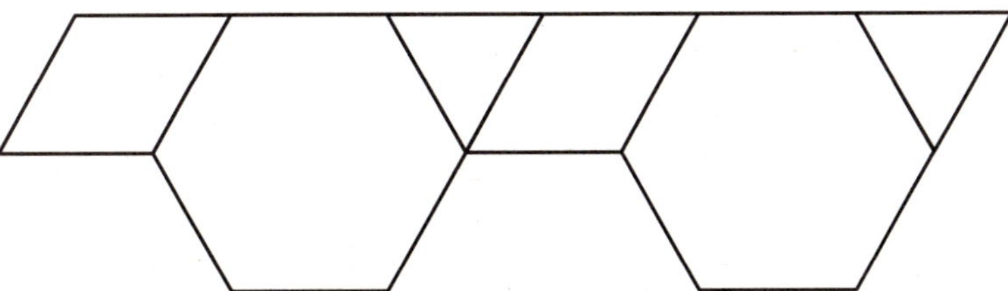

__________ __________

3.

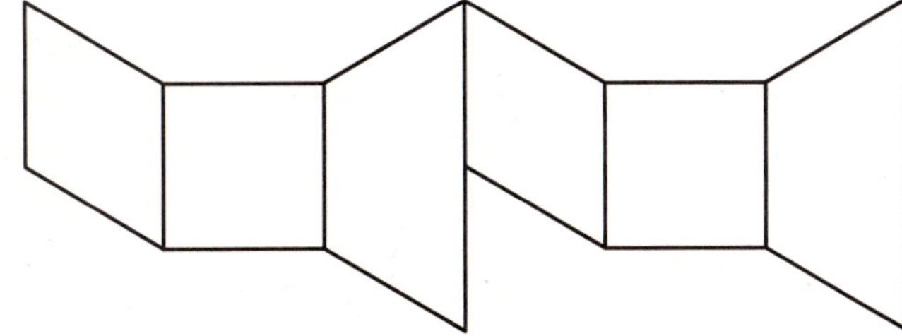

__________ __________ __________

Say It

How many different shapes are used in each pattern? Name the patterns.

0-7424-1928-2 *Patterns*

Name ______________________ Date ______________

ABC Patterns

Directions: Use pattern blocks to make the pattern. Then answer the questions.

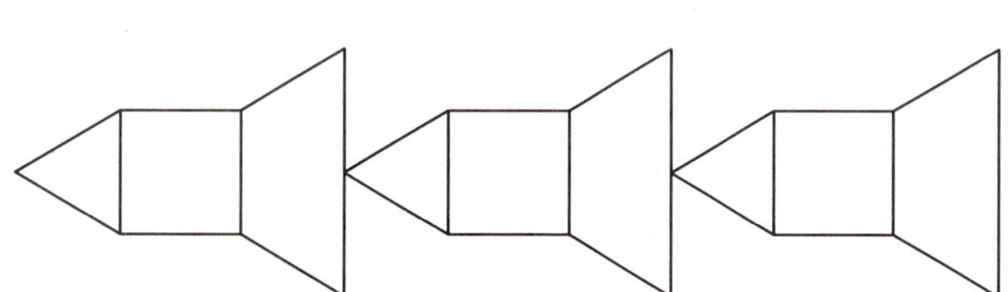

1. How many blocks make one rocket? ______________

2. How many different shapes were used? ______________

3. If the pattern continues, what shape will be next? ______________

4. What shape will the 12th block be? ______________

5. What shape will the 14th block be? ______________

Say It

Make your own pattern. Don't let your partner see it.
Tell your partner about the pattern. See if your partner can copy the pattern.

Name ________________________________ Date ____________________

Other Patterns

Directions: Use pattern blocks to make the pattern. Then answer the questions.

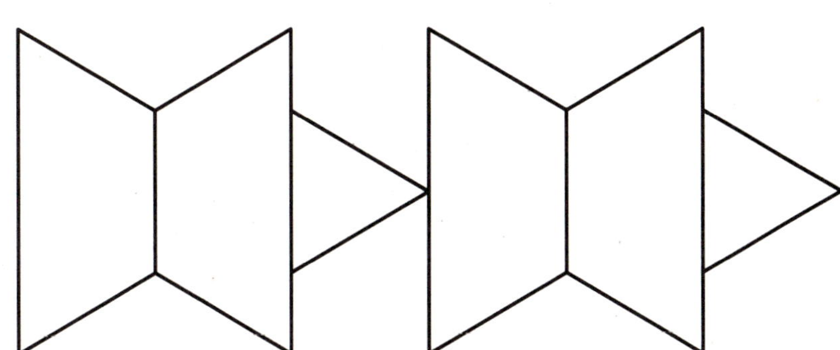

1. How many blocks make one butterfly? ____________________

2. How many different shapes were used? ____________________

3. If the pattern continues, what shape will be next? ____________________

4. What shape will the 9th block be? ____________________

5. What shape will the 10th block be? ____________________

Say It

Make your own pattern. Don't let your partner see it.
Tell your partner about the pattern. See if your partner can copy the pattern.

Name ______________________ Date ______________

Other Patterns

Directions: Use pattern blocks to make the pattern. Then answer the questions.

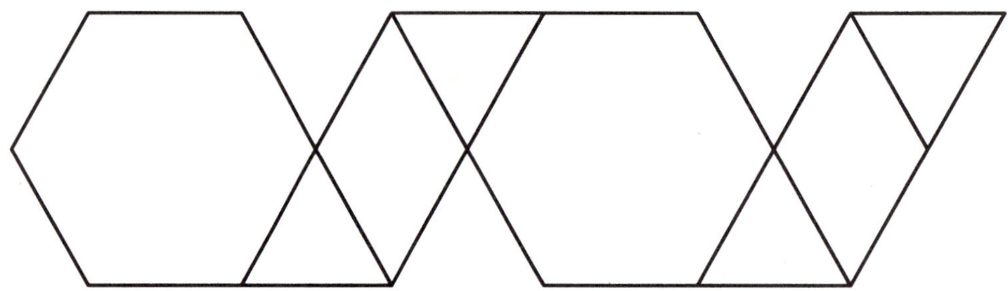

1. How many blocks are used before the pattern repeats? ____________

2. How many different shapes are used? ____________

3. If the pattern continues, what shape will be next? ____________

4. What shape will the 12th block be? ____________

5. What shape will the 14th block be? ____________

Say It

Make your own pattern. Don't let your partner see it.
Tell your partner about the pattern. See if your partner can copy the pattern.

Name ______________________ Date ______________

Vertical Patterns

Directions: Each pattern is different. Color the camels. Complete the patterns. R = Red, G = Green, B = Blue, Y = Yellow O = Orange, P = Purple.

1.

2.

3.

Say It

Name each pattern. Use claps and stomps to copy each pattern.

Name ______________________ Date ______________

Vertical Patterns

Directions: Match the letter pattern. Draw stripes on cats.

A means stripes.  **B** means no stripes. 

1.

A 

B 

A 

B 

A

B 

2.

A 

B 

B 

A 

B 

B 

 **Say It**

Say each pattern out loud. Use the words **stripes** and **no stripes**.

0-7424-1928-2 *Patterns*

Name ______________________________ Date ______________

Table Patterns

Directions: Color the penguins' stomachs. Complete the pattern.
G = Green, B = Blue, R = Red

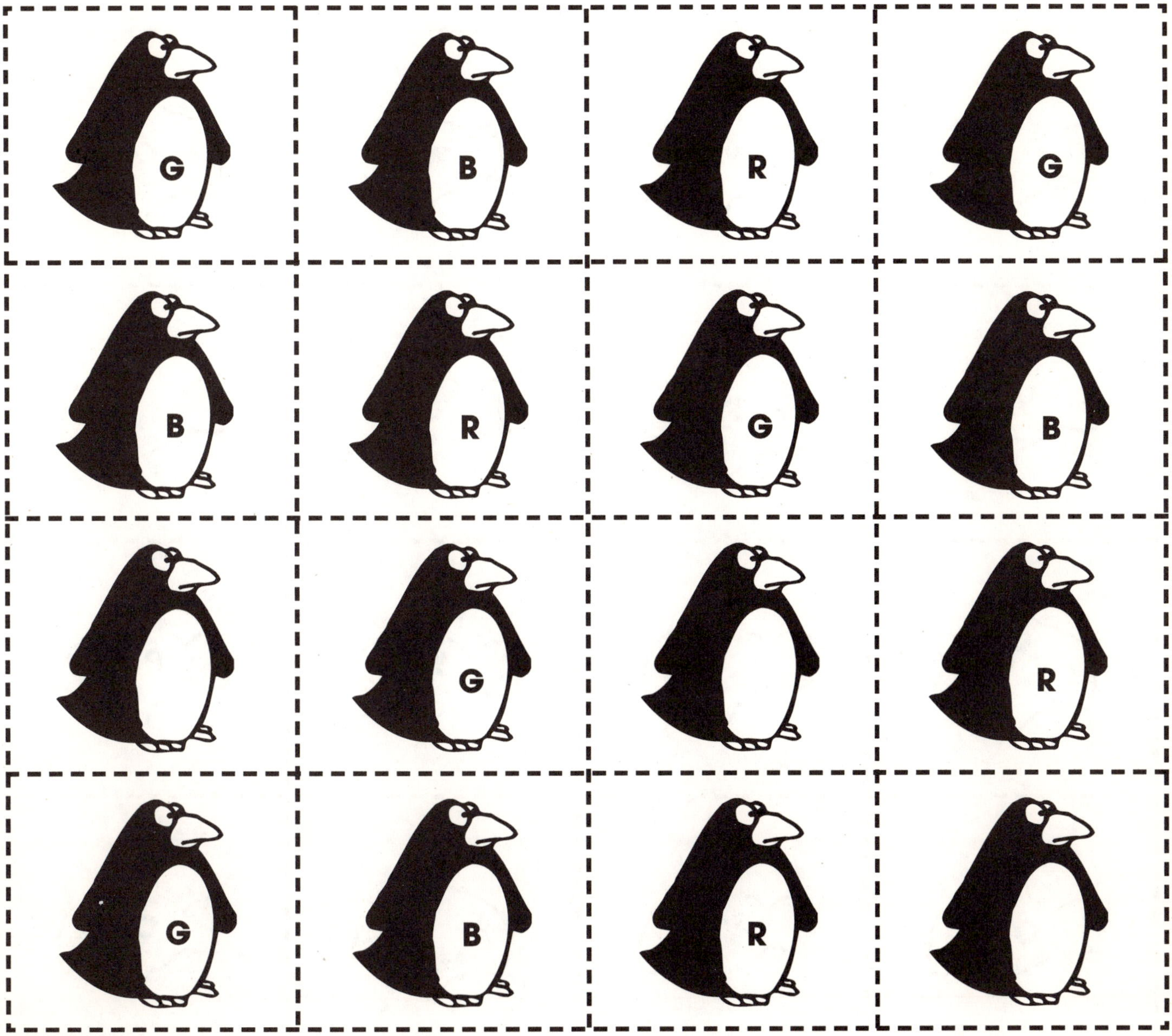

G	B	R	G
B	R	G	B
	G		R
G	B	R	

Say It

What is the pattern if you read the table from left to right?
What is the pattern if you read the table from up to down?
What is the pattern going diagonally?

Name ______________________________ Date ____________________

Table Patterns

Directions: Color the fish. Complete the pattern.
Y = Yellow, P = Purple, O = Orange

	Y	P	O
Y	P	O	
P		Y	P
O	Y		O

Say It

What is the pattern if you read the table from left to right?
What is the pattern if you read the table from up to down?
What is the pattern going diagonally?

Name ______________________ Date ______________

1 More

Directions: Find the pattern. Complete the table. Answer the questions.

Number of Mice	Number of Tails
	1
	2

1. How many mice are there in all? ________

2. How many tails do they have in all? ________

3. 10 mice = ________ tails

Say It

Tell how the pattern for the number of tails grows.

Name ______________________ Date ______________

1 More

Directions: Use paper cups to build the pyramids. Complete the table. Find the pattern.

2 cups on the bottom = 2 layers high

3 cups on the bottom = 3 layers high

4 cups on the bottom = 4 layers high

Number of Cups on Bottom	Number of Layers
2	2
3	3
4	
5	
6	

Say It

How is this pattern the same as the pattern on page 25? How is it different?

Name ______________________ Date ______________

1 More

Directions: Read the story. Complete the table. Draw the apples. Write the number.

Farmer Thompson grows apples. He has many children to help pick apples. The farmer has 3 apples. Each child brings him 1 more apple.

Number of Children	Number of Apples
0	🍎🍎🍎 3
1	🍎🍎🍎🍎 4
2	🍎🍎🍎🍎🍎
3	
4	
5	

Say It

What part of the story tells how the pattern will grow?

0-7424-1928-2 *Patterns*

Name ______________________ Date ______________

2 More

Directions: Find the pattern. Complete the table. Answer the questions.

Number of Rabbits	Number of Ears
🐇	2
🐇 🐇	4
🐇 🐇 🐇	
🐇 🐇 🐇 🐇	
🐇 🐇 🐇 🐇 🐇	

1. Does the pattern grow or decrease? __________

2. How does the pattern change each time? ______________________________

3. How many ears on 9 rabbits? __________

Say It

Color the *Number of Ears* pattern on a 100 chart. Say the numbers out loud as you color. Make up a question about the number of rabbits and the number of ears.

0-7424-1928-2 *Patterns*

Name ______________________ Date ______________

2 More

Directions: Use cubes to build the chair. Complete the table.

The chair 2 cubes tall takes 3 cubes to build.

The chair 3 cubes tall takes 5 cubes to build.

The chair 4 cubes tall takes 7 cubes to build.

Height of Chair	Number of Cubes
2	3
3	5
4	7
5	
6	

1. Does the pattern grow or decrease? ______________

2. How does the number of cubes change each time the chair gets taller? ______________________________

3. How many cubes to build a chair 10 cubes high? ______________

Say It

How is this pattern the same as the pattern on page 28? How is it different?

0-7424-1928-2 *Patterns*

Name ______________________________ Date ______________

2 More

Directions: Read the story. Complete the table.

Each lily pad has 2 frogs on it.

If there is 1 lily pad, there will be 2 frogs.

If there are 2 lily pads, there will be 4 frogs.

If there are 3 lily pads, there will be 6 frogs.

Lilly Pads	Number of Frogs
1	2
2	4
3	6
4	
5	
6	

Directions: Color the *Number of Frogs* pattern on a 100 chart. Continue the pattern. Answer the questions.

1. How many frogs will be on 10 lily pads? __________

2. How many frogs will be on 20 lily pads? __________

3. How many lily pads will hold 50 frogs? __________

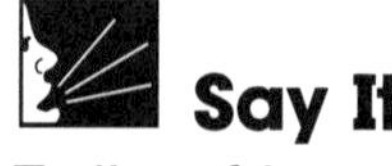

Say It

Tell a friend how using a 100 chart helped you answer the questions.

0-7424-1928-2 *Patterns*

Name ______________________________ Date ______________

3 More

Directions: Use pattern blocks to make cats. Answer the questions.

1. How many blocks to make 1 cat? __________

2. How many blocks to make 2 cats? __________

3. How many blocks to make 3 cats? __________

Directions: Find the pattern. Complete the table.

Number of Cats	Number of Blocks
1	
2	
3	
4	
5	

Say It

Color the *Number of Blocks* pattern on a 100 chart. Say the numbers out loud as you color. Make up a question about the number of blocks and the number of cats.

0-7424-1928-2 *Patterns*

Name ______________________ Date ______________

3 More

Directions: Use cubes to build the models. Complete the table. Answer the questions.

A building with 1 floor takes 3 cubes to build.

A building with 2 floors takes 6 cubes to build.

A building with 3 floors takes 9 cubes to build.

Number of Floors	Number of Cubes
1	3
2	6
3	9
4	
5	

1. Does the pattern grow or decrease? __________

2. How does the pattern change each time? ______________________________

3. How many cubes will it take to make a building with 10 floors? __________

Say It

How is this pattern the same as the one on page 31? How is it different?

Name ______________________________ Date ____________________

3 More

Directions: Look at the table. Find the pattern. Complete the table.

Number of Ducks	Number of Ducklings
1	3
2	6
3	9
4	
5	
6	

Directions: Fill in the blanks to make a story that matches the pattern in the table.

Ducks are __________ in a pond. Each mother duck has __________ ducklings. If there is 1 mother duck, then there are __________ ducklings. If there are 2 mother ducks, then there are __________ ducklings. If Tori counts 10 mother ducks, then there are __________ ducklings.

Say It

Describe the *Number of Ducklings* pattern to a friend.

Name ______________________________ Date ______________

4 More

Directions: Cut out the turtles at the bottom of the page. Paste the correct number of turtles in the table. Write the correct numeral in the *Number of Legs* column.

Number of Turtles	Number of Legs
1 ☐	
2 ☐ ☐	
3 ☐ ☐ ☐	

Say It

Color the *Number of Legs* pattern on a 100 chart. Continue the pattern. Say the numbers out loud as you color. Make up a question about the number of turtles and the number of legs.

Name ______________________ Date ______________

4 More

Directions: Use cubes to build the arches. Complete the table. Answer the questions.

I arch takes 7 cubes to build.

2 arches take 11 cubes to build.

3 arches take 15 cubes to build.

Number of Arches	Number of Cubes
1	7
2	11
3	15
4	
5	

1. Does the pattern grow or decrease? __________

2. How does the number of cubes change each time an arch is added?

____

3. How many cubes will be needed to build 8 arches? __________

Say It

How is this pattern the same as the one on page 34? How is it different?

Name ______________________ Date ______________

5 More

Directions: Use toothpicks to build the hexagons. Complete the table.

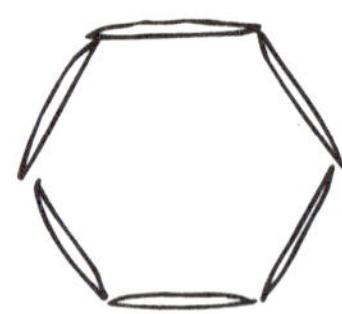

1 hexagon takes 6 toothpicks to build.

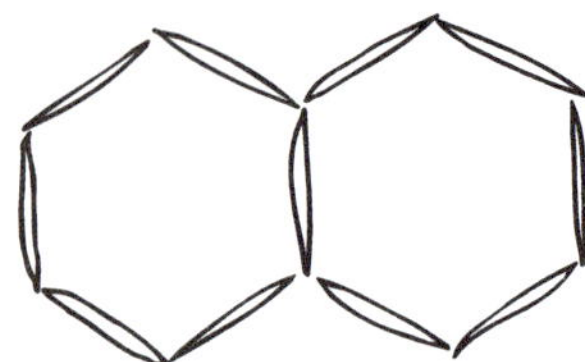

2 hexagons take 11 toothpicks to build.

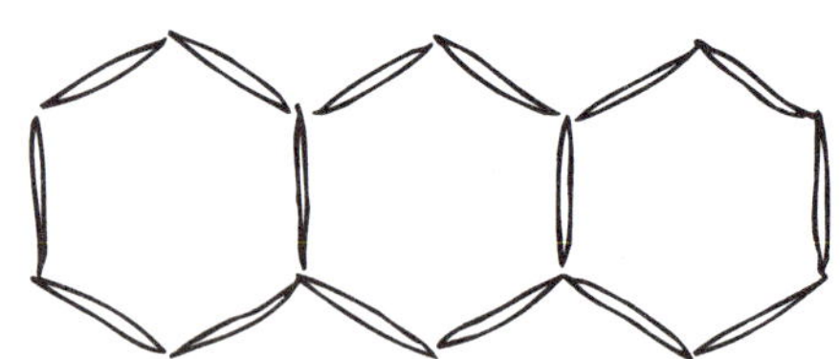

3 hexagons take 16 toothpicks to build.

Number of Hexagons	Number of Toothpicks
1	6
2	11
3	16
4	
5	

Say It

Color the *Number of Toothpicks* pattern on a 100 chart. Continue the pattern. Say the pattern out loud. Make up a question about the number of hexagons and the number of toothpicks.

Name ______________________ Date ______________

8 More

Directions: Find the pattern. Complete the table.

Number of Spiders	Number of Legs
(1 spider)	8
(2 spiders)	
(3 spiders)	
(4 spiders)	
(5 spiders)	

Directions: Color the *Number of Legs* pattern on a 100 chart. Continue the pattern. Answer the questions.

1. How many legs are on 8 spiders? ________

2. How many legs are on 10 spiders? ________

3. How many spiders would have 56 legs? ________

Say It

Tell a friend how using a 100 chart helped you answer the questions.

0-7424-1928-2 *Patterns*

Name ______________________ Date ______________

10 More

Directions: Find the pattern. Complete the table.

Number of People	Number of Toes
(1 person)	10
(2 people)	
(3 people)	
(4 people)	
(5 people)	

Directions: Color the *Number of Toes* pattern on a 100 chart. Continue the pattern. Answer the questions.

1. How many toes are on 8 people? __________

2. How many toes are on 10 people? __________

3. How many people would have 90 toes? __________

Say It

Tell a friend how using a 100 chart helped you answer the questions.

Name ______________________________ Date ______________________

2 Less

Directions: Read the story. Complete the table. Answer the questions.

Mrs. McGillis has a lot of cats. They are napping in the house. One by one, each cat gets up and goes outside to play. Each cat has 2 ears.

Number of Cats in the House	Number of Ears
	10

1. Does the *Number of Ears* pattern grow or decrease? ______________

2. What happens to the number of ears each time a cat leaves?

____

3. What part of the story tells you how the pattern will change?

____

Say It

How is this pattern similar to the one on page 28? How is it different?

0-7424-1928-2 *Patterns*

Name ______________________ Date ______________

3 Less

Directions: Read the story. Complete the table. Answer the questions.

There are 5 nests in the nature center. Each nest has 3 eggs. The park rangers need to move the nests to a safer place. They move 1 nest at a time.

Number of Nests	Total Number of Eggs
	15

1. Does the *Number of Eggs* pattern grow or decrease? ______________

2. What happens to the number of eggs each time a nest is moved?

____

3. What part of the story tells you how the pattern will change?

____

Say It

Use a 100 chart. Start at the number 50. Color a *3 less* pattern on the chart. Make up a story to match your pattern.

0-7424-1928-2 *Patterns*

Name ______________________________ Date ______________

4 Less

Directions: Use square pattern blocks to build the windmills. Find the pattern. Complete the table.

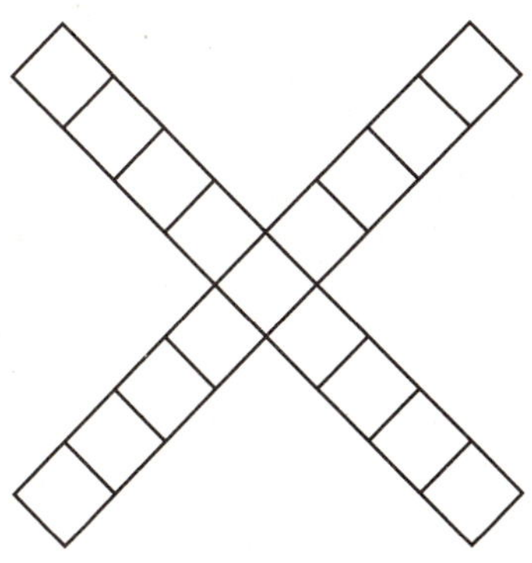

1st windmill

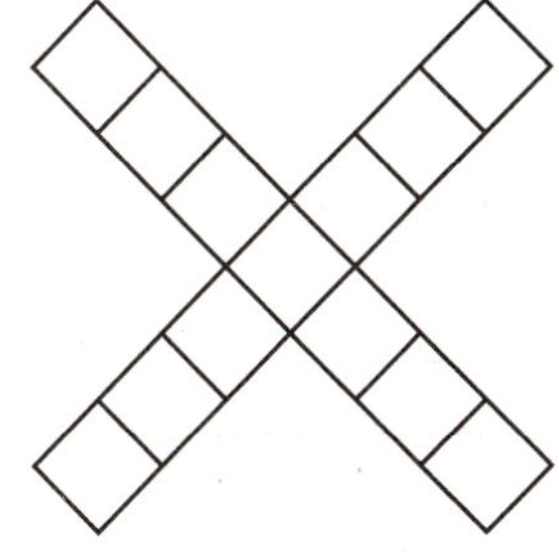

2nd windmill

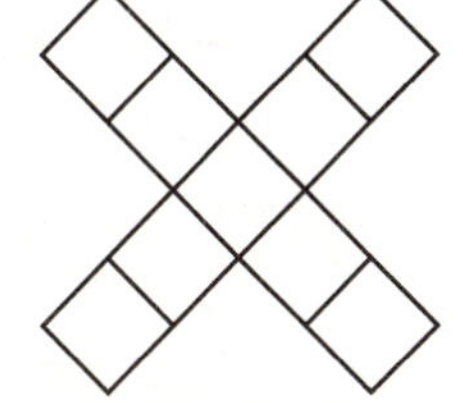

3rd windmill

Windmill	Number of Squares
1st	17
2nd	
3rd	
4th	

Say It

Describe the *Number of Squares* pattern to a partner.

Name ______________________ Date ______________

5 Less

Directions: Read the story. Find the pattern. Complete the table. Answer the questions.

There are 5 hands raised in the air. Each hand has 5 fingers. When the teacher calls on a student, 1 hand is put down.

Number of Hands in the Air	Number of Fingers
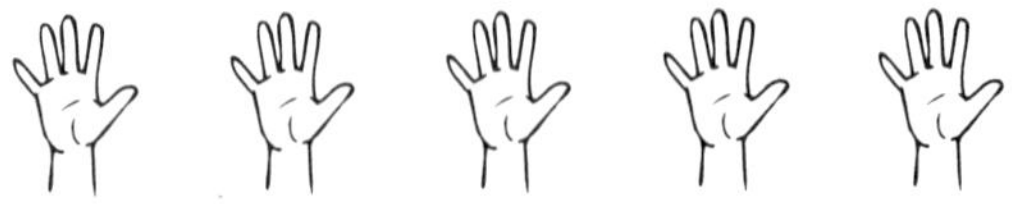	25
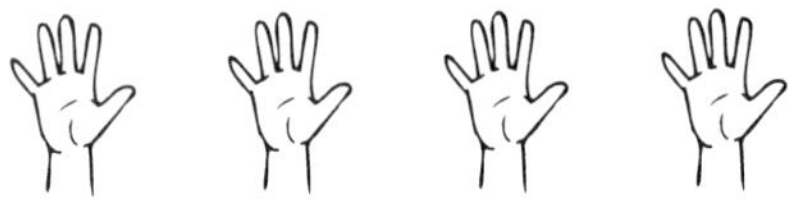	
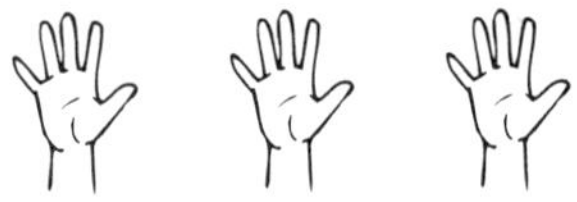	
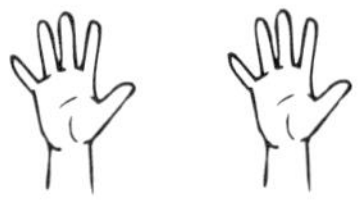	
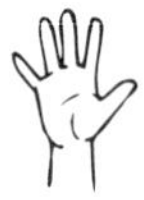	

1. What happens to the number of fingers each time 1 hand is put down?

____

2. Does this pattern grow or decrease? ______________________

3. How would the pattern be different if it started with 10 hands raised?

____

Say It

Use a 100 chart. Start at the number 50. Color a *5 less* pattern. Say the numbers out loud.

Name ______________________________ Date ______________

6 Less

Directions: Use pattern blocks to build the suns. Find the pattern. Complete the table.

4 layers = 24 rays

3 layers = ________ rays

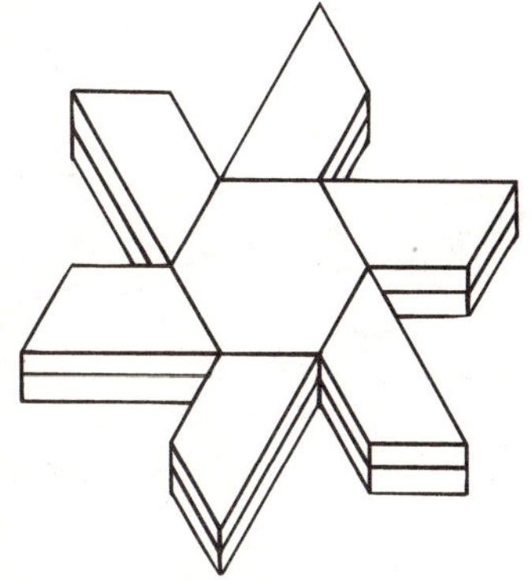

2 layers = ________ rays

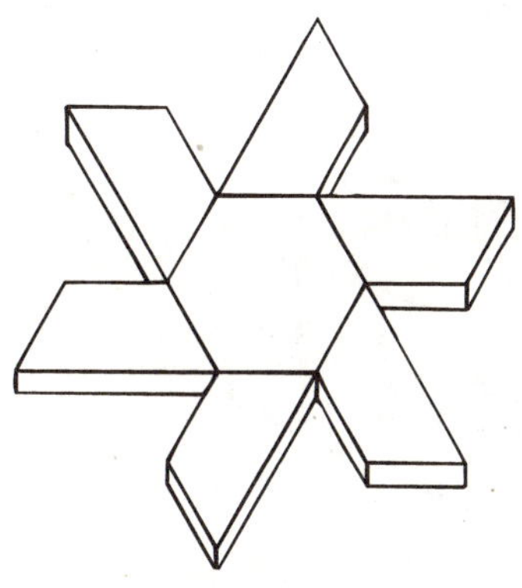

1 layer = ________ rays

Number of Layers	Number of Rays
4	24
3	
2	
1	

Say It

Use a 100 chart to color the *Number of Rays* pattern. Describe the pattern to a friend.

Name ____________________ Date ____________

8 Less

Directions: Use cubes to build the wells. Find the pattern. Complete the table.

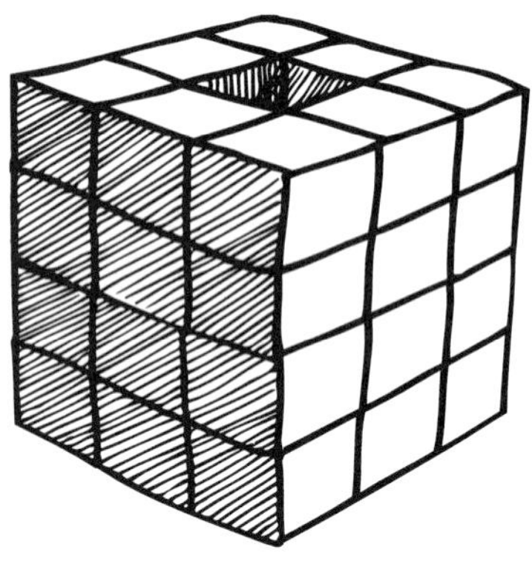

4 layers = 32 cubes

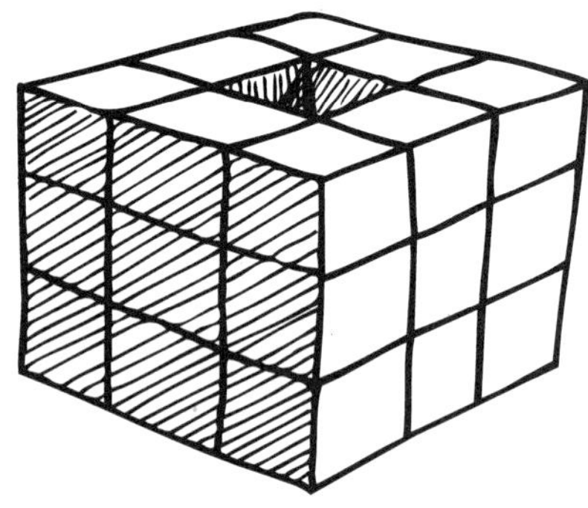

3 layers = ________ cubes

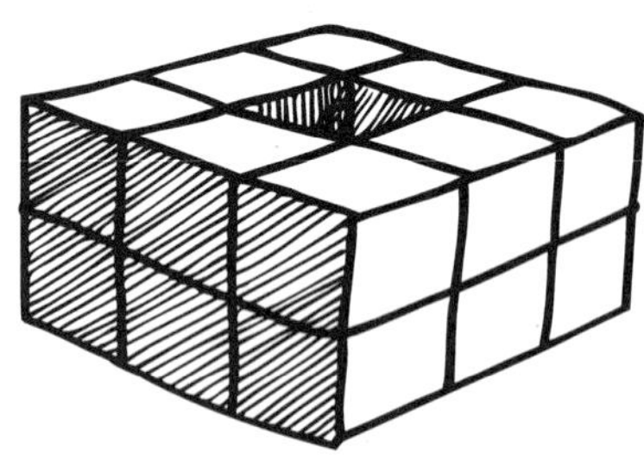

2 layers = ________ cubes

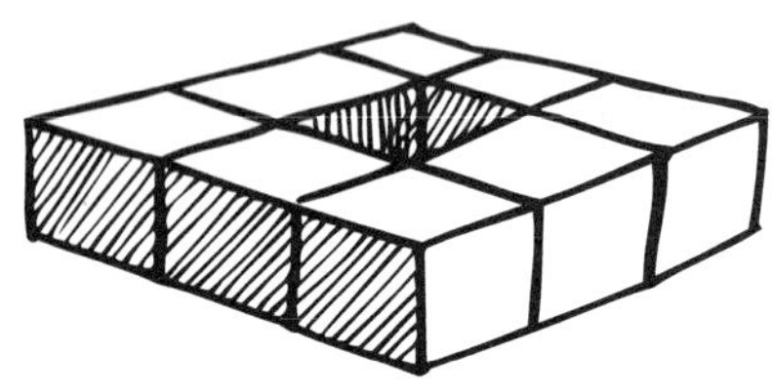

1 layer = ________ cubes

Number of Layers	Number of Cubes
4	32
3	
2	
1	

Say It

Use a 100 chart to color the *Number of Cubes* pattern. Describe the pattern to a friend.

Name ______________________________ Date ______________________

Pattern Blocks

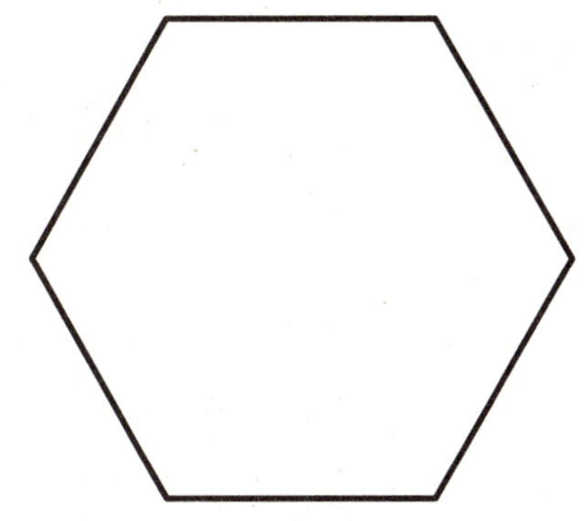
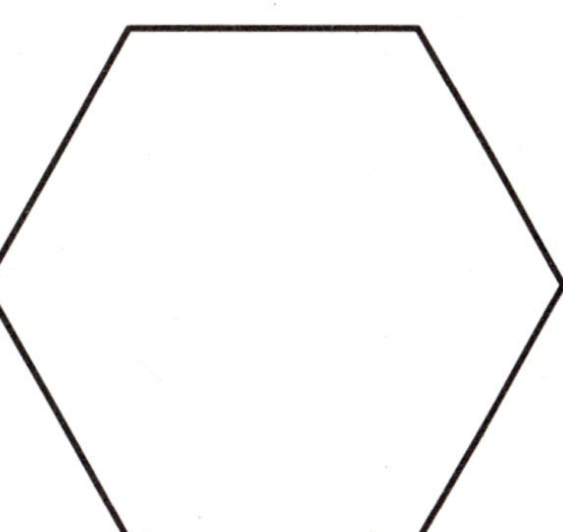
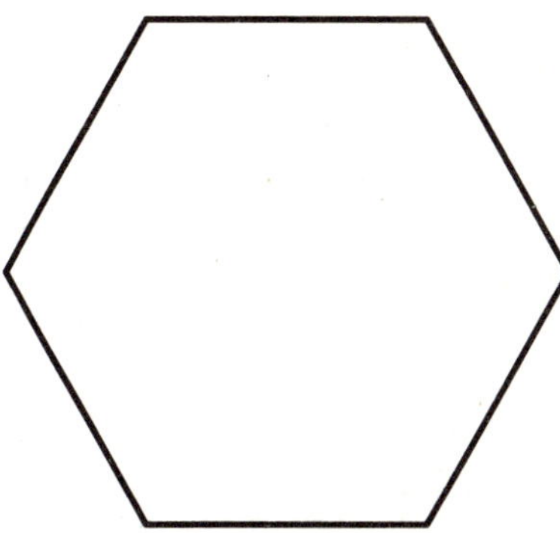

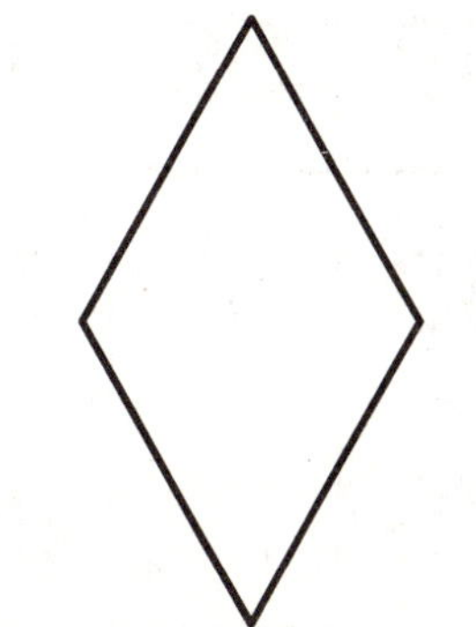
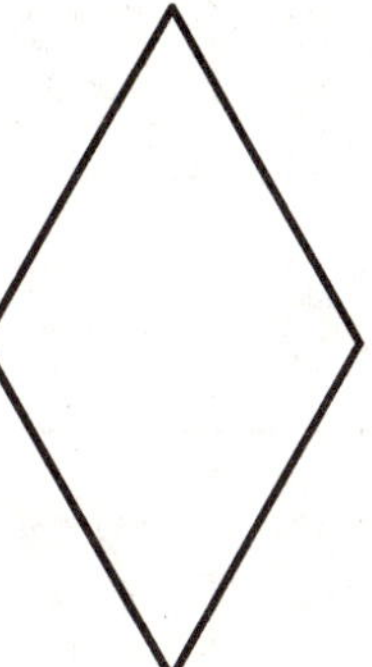
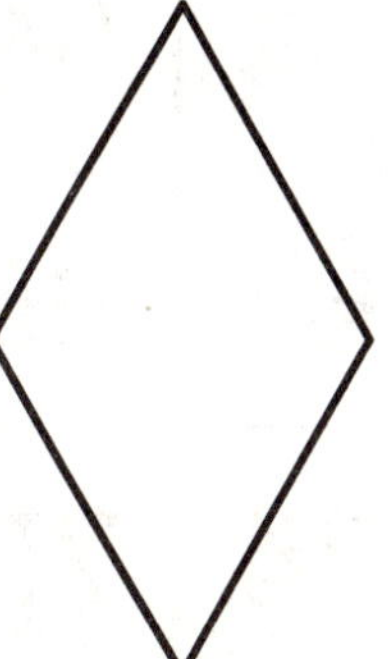
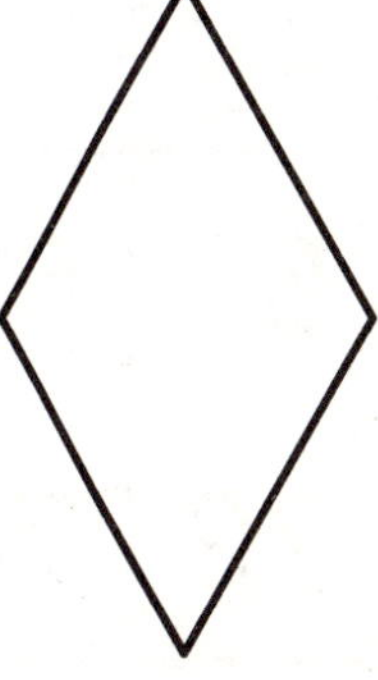

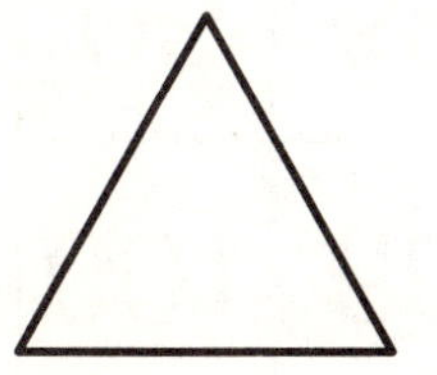
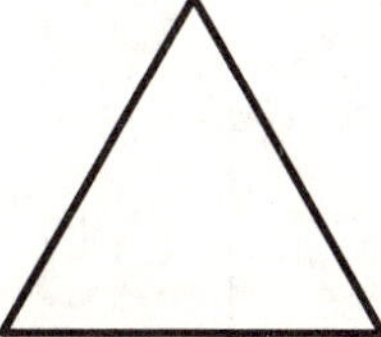
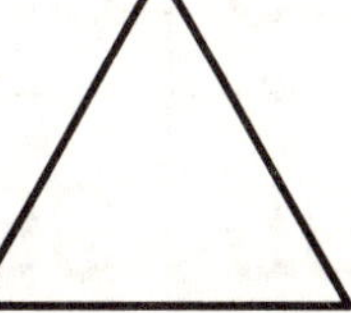
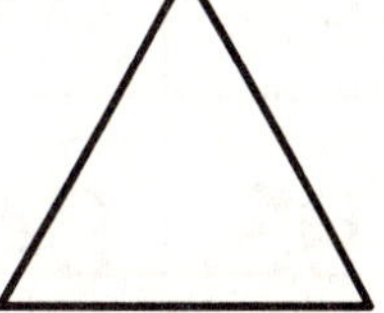
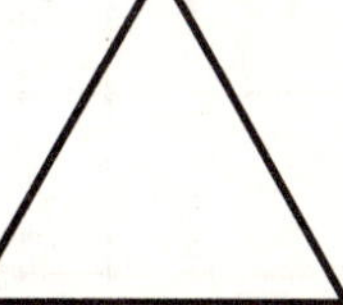

Name ______________________ Date ______________

100 Chart

1	2	3	4	5	6	7	8	9	10
11	12	13	14	15	16	17	18	19	20
21	22	23	24	25	26	27	28	29	30
31	32	33	34	35	36	37	38	39	40
41	42	43	44	45	46	47	48	49	50
51	52	53	54	55	56	57	58	59	60
61	62	63	64	65	66	67	68	69	70
71	72	73	74	75	76	77	78	79	80
81	82	83	84	85	86	87	88	89	90
91	92	93	94	95	96	97	98	99	100

Answer Key

page 4
1. G Y G Y G Y
2. Y G Y G Y G
3. R B R B R B

page 5
1. large, small, large, small, large, small
2. type 1, type 2, type 1, type 2, type 1, type 2
3. happy, sad, happy, sad, happy, sad

page 6
1. A B A B A
2. A B A B A B
3. Answers will vary.

page 7
1. A B A B
2. A B A B A B
3. Answers will vary.

page 8
1. triangle, parallelogram
2. trapezoid, parallelogram
3. square, triangle

page 9
1. stomp, clap, clap (repeat)
2. hands up, hands angled, hands angled (repeat)
3. kick left, kick right, kick right (repeat)

page 10
1. R B B R B B
2. B B R B B R
3. O P P O P P

page 11
1. hexagon, triangle
2. triangle, parallelogram
3. triangle, triangle

page 12
1. baseball cap, baseball cap, cowboy hat, cowboy hat, baseball cap, baseball cap
2. sneakers, sneakers, loafers, loafers, sneakers, sneakers
3. small, small, large, large, small, small

page 13
1. stomp, stomp, clap, clap (repeat)
2. hands up, hands up, hands angled, hands angled (repeat)
3. jump, jump, sit, sit (repeat)

page 14
1. rock, paper, scissors, rock, paper, scissors
2. paper, scissors, rock, paper, scissors, rock
3. paper, rock, scissors, paper, rock, scissors

page 15
1. large, medium, small, large, medium, small
2. medium, large, small, medium, large, small
3. small, medium, large, small, medium, large

page 16
1. A B C A B C
2. A B C A B C
3. Answers will vary.

page 17
1. hexagon
2. parallelogram, hexagon
3. parallelogram, square, trapezoid

page 18
1. 3
2. 3
3. triangle
4. trapezoid
5. square

page 19
1. 3
2. 2
3. trapezoid
4. triangle
5. trapezoid

page 20
1. 4
2. 3
3. hexagon
4. triangle
5. triangle

page 21
1. R G G R G G
2. B B Y Y B B
3. O P P O P P

page 22
1. stripes, no stripes, stripes, no stripes, stripes, no stripes
2. stripes, no stripes, no stripes, stripes, no stripes, no stripes

Answer Key

page 23
G B R G
B R G B
R G B R
G B R G

page 24
O Y P O
Y P O Y
P O Y P
O Y P O

page 25
Number of Tails = 1, 2, 3, 4, 5
1. 15 mice
2. 15 tails
3. 10 tails

page 26
Number of Layers = 2, 3, 4, 5, 6

page 27
Number of Apples = 3, 4, 5, 6, 7, 8

page 28
Number of Ears = 2, 4, 6, 8, 10
1. grow
2. 2 more ears are added for each rabbit
3. 18 ears

page 29
Number of Cubes = 3, 5, 7, 9, 11
1. grow
2. add 2 cubes each time height goes up by 1
3. 19 cubes

page 30
Number of Frogs = 2, 4, 6, 8, 10, 12
1. 20 frogs
2. 40 frogs
3. 25 lily pads

page 31
1. 3 blocks
2. 6 blocks
3. 9 blocks
Number of Blocks = 3, 6, 9, 12, 15

page 32
Number of Cubes = 3, 6, 9, 12, 15
1. grow
2. add 3 cubes for every floor
3. 30 cubes

page 33
Number of Ducklings = 3, 6, 9, 12, 15, 18
swimming; 3; 3; 6; 30

page 34
Number of Legs = 4, 8, 12

page 35
Number of Cubes = 7, 11, 15, 19, 23
1. grow
2. add 4 cubes for each arch
3. 35 cubes

page 36
Number of Toothpicks = 6, 11, 16, 21, 26

page 37
Number of Legs = 8, 16, 24, 32, 40
1. 64 legs
2. 80 legs
3. 7 spiders

page 38
Number of Toes = 10, 20, 30, 40, 50
1. 80 toes
2. 100 toes
3. 9 people

page 39
Number of Ears = 10, 8, 6, 4, 2
1. decrease
2. number of ears goes down by 2
3. Each cat has 2 ears. The cats leave one by one.

page 40
Total Number of Eggs = 15, 12, 9, 6, 3
1. decrease
2. goes down by 3
3. Each nest has 3 eggs. They move 1 nest at a time.

page 41
Number of Squares = 17, 13, 9, 5

page 42
Number of Fingers = 25, 20, 15, 10, 5
1. goes down by 5
2. decrease
3. There would be 50 fingers to start. The counting pattern would be the same.

page 43
Number of Rays = 24, 18, 12, 6

page 44
Number of Cubes = 32, 24, 16, 8